Y0-ABH-937

8-20-70

ASPECTS OF MODERN OPERA

ASPECTS OF MODERN OPERA

Estimates and Inquiries

BY

LAWRENCE GILMAN

AUTHOR OF

"The Music of To-morrow," "Phases of Modern Music," "Stories of Symphonic Music," "Edward MacDowell: A Study," "Strauss' 'Salome': A Guide to the Opera," "Debussy's 'Pelléas et Mélisande': A Guide to the Opera," etc.

HASKELL HOUSE PUBLISHERS LTD.

Publishers of Scarce Scholarly Books

NEW YORK, N. Y. 10012

1969

First Published 1909

HASKELL HOUSE PUBLISHERS LTD.
Publishers of Scarce Scholarly Books
280 LAFAYETTE STREET
NEW YORK, N. Y. 10012

Library of Congress Catalog Card Number: 68-25288

Standard Book Number 8383-0302-1

Printed in the United States of America

TO

ERNEST NEWMAN

A CRITIC OF

BREADTH, WISDOM, AND INDEPENDENCE

THESE STUDIES

ARE APPRECIATIVELY INSCRIBED

CONTENTS

INTRODUCTORY

THE WAGNERIAN AFTER-MATH

INTRODUCTORY

THE WAGNERIAN AFTERMATH

SINCE that day when, a quarter of a century ago, Richard Wagner ceased to be a dynamic figure in the life of the world, the history of operatic art has been, save for a few conspicuous exceptions, a barren and unprofitable page; and it has been so, in a considerable degree, because of him. When Mr. William F. Apthorp, in his admirable history of the opera — a book written with unflagging gusto and vividness—observed that Wagner's style has been, since his death, little imitated, he made an astonishing assertion. "If by Wagner's influence," he went on, "is meant the influence of his individuality, it may fairly be said to have been null. In this respect Wagner has had no more followers than Mozart or Beethoven; he has founded no school." Again one must exclaim: An astonishing affirmation! and it is not the first time that it has been made, nor will it be the last. Yet how it can have seemed a reasonable thing to say is one of the insoluble mysteries. The influence of Wagner — the influence of his individuality as well as of his principles — upon the musical art of the past twenty-five years has been simply incalculable. It has tinged, when it has not dyed and saturated, every phase and form of creative music, from the opera to the sonata and string quartet.

It is not easy to understand how anyone who is at all familiar with the products of musical art in Europe and America since the death of the tyrant of Bayreuth can be disposed to question the fact. No composer who ever lived influenced so deeply the music that came after him as did Wagner. It is an influence that is, of course, waning; and to the definite good of creative art, for it has been in a large degree pernicious and oppressive in its effect. The shadow of the most pervasive of modern masters has laid a sinister and paralysing magic upon almost all of his successors. They have sought to exert his spells, they have muttered what they imagined were his incantations; yet the thing which they had hoped to raise up in glory and in strength has stubbornly refused to breathe with any save an artificial and feeble life. None has escaped the contagion of his genius, though some, whom we shall later discuss, have opposed against it a genius and a creative passion of their own. Yet in the domain of the opera, wherewith we are here especially concerned, it is an exceedingly curious and interesting fact that out of the soil which he enriched with his own genius have sprung, paradoxically, the only living and independent forces in the lyrico-dramatic art of our time.

Let us consider, first, those aspects of the operatic situation which, by reason of the paucity of creative vitality that they connote, are, to-day, most striking; and here we shall be obliged to turn at once to Germany. The more one hears of the new music that is being put forth by Teutonic composers, the stronger grows one's conviction of the lack, with a single exception, of any genuine creative impulse in that country to-day. It is doubtless a little unreasonable to expect to be able to agree in this matter with the amiable lady who told Matthew Arnold that she liked to think that æsthetic excellence was "common and abundant." As the sagacious Arnold pointed out, it is not in the nature of æsthetic excellence that it should be "common and abundant"; on the contrary, he observed, excellence dwells among rocks hardly accessible, and a man must almost wear out his heart before he can reach her. All of this is quite unanswerable; yet, so far as musical Germany is concerned, is not the situation rather singular? Germany — the Germany which yielded the royal line founded by Bach and continued by Mozart, Beethoven, Schubert, Schumann, Wagner, and Brahms — can show us to-day, save for that exception which we shall later discuss, only a strenuous flock of Lilliputians (whom it would be fatuous to discuss with particularity), each one of whom is confidently aware that the majestic mantle of the author of "Tristan" has descended upon himself. They write music in which one grows weary of finding the same delinquency—the invariable fault of emptiness, of poverty of idea, allied with an extreme elaboration in the manner of presentation. And it is most deliberate and determined in address. One would think that the message about to be delivered were of the utmost consequence, the deepest moment: the pose and the manner of the bearer of great tidings are admirably simulated. Yet the actual deliverance is futile and dull, pathetically meagre, causing us to wonder how often we must remind ourselves that it is as impossible to achieve salient or distinguished or noble music without salient, distinguished, and noble ideas as it is to create fire without flame.

In France there are — again with an exception to which we shall later advert — Saint-Saëns, d'Indy, Massenet, Charpentier, and — *les autres*.

Now Saint-Saëns is very far from being a Wagnerian. He is, indeed, nothing very definite and determinable. He is M. Saint-Saëns, an abstraction, a brain without a personality. It is almost forty years since Hector Berlioz called him "one of the greatest musicians of our epoch," and since then the lustre of his fame has waxed steadily, until to-day one must recognise him as one of the three or four most distinguished living composers. Venerable and urbane, M. Saint-Saëns, at the New York opening of the American tour which he made in his seventy-second year, sat at the piano before the audience whom he had travelled three thousand miles to meet, and played a virtuoso piece with orchestral accompaniment, and two shorter pieces for piano and orchestra: a valse-caprice called "Wedding Cake," and an "Allegro Appassionato." That is to say, M. Camille Saint-Saëns, the bearer of an internationally famous and most dignified name, braved the tragic perils of the deep to exhibit himself before a representative American audience as the composer of the "Wedding Cake" valse-caprice, an entertaining fantasy on exotic folk-themes, and a *jeu d'esprit* with a pleasant tune and some pretty orchestral embroidery.

No one could have it in his heart

to chide M. Saint-Saëns for these things, for he is very venerable and very famous. Yet is not the occurrence indicative, in a way, of M. Saint Saëns's own attitude toward his art? —that facile, brilliant, admirably competent, chameleon-like art of his, so adroit in its external fashioning, yet so thin and worn in its inner substance! One wonders if, in the entire history of music, there is the record of a composer more completely accomplished in his art, so exquisite a master of the difficult trick of spinning a musical web, so superb a mechanician, who has less to say to the world: whose discourse is so meagre and so negligible. One remembers that unfortunate encomium of Gounod's, which has been so often turned into a justified reproach: "Saint Saëns," said the composer of "Faust," "will write at will a work in the style of Rossini, of Verdi, of Schumann, of Wagner." The pity of his case is that, when he writes pure Saint-Saëns, one does not greatly care to listen. He has spoken no musical thought, in all his long and scintillant career, that the world will long remember. His dozen operas, his symphonic poems, his symphonies, his concertos, the best of his chamber works — is there in them an accent which one can soberly call either eloquent or deeply beautiful? Do they not excel solely by reason of their symmetry and solidity of structure, their deft and ingenious delivery of ideas which at their worst are banal and at their best mediocre or derivative? "A name always to be remembered with respect!" cries one of his most sane and just admirers: since "in the face of practical difficulties, discouragements, misunderstandings, sneers, he has worked constantly to the best of his unusual ability for musical righteousness in its pure form."

"A name to be remembered with respect," beyond dispute: with the respect that is due the man of supereminent intelligence, the fastidious artisan, the tireless and honourable workman—with respect, yes; but scarcely with enthusiasm. He never, as has been truly said, bores one; it is just as true that he never stimulates, moves, transports, or delights one, in the deeper sense of the term. At its best, it is a hard and dry light that shines out of his music: a radiance without magic and without warmth. His work is an impressive monument to the futility of art without impulse: to the immeasurable distance that separates the most exquisite talent from the merest genius. For all its brilliancy of investiture, his thought, as the most liberal of his appreciators has said, "can never wander through eternity"—a truth which scarcely needed the invocation of the Miltonic line to enforce. It may be true, as Mr. Philip Hale has asserted, that "the success of d'Indy, Fauré, Debussy, was made possible by the labor and the talent of Saint-Saëns"; yet it is one of the pities of his case that when Saint-Saëns's name shall have become faint and fugitive in the corridors of time, the chief glories of French art in our day will be held to be, one may venture, the legacies of the composers of "Pelléas et Mélisande" and the "Jour d'été à la montagne," rather than of the author of "Samson et Dalila" and "Le Rouet d'Omphale." Which brings one to M. Vincent d'Indy.

Now M. d'Indy offers a curious spectacle to the inquisitive observer, in that he is, in one regard, the very symbol of independence, of artistic emancipation, whereas, in another phase of his activity, he is a mere echo and simulacrum. As a writer for the concert room, as a composer of imaginative orchestral works and of chamber music, he is one of the most inflexibly original and self-guided composers known to the contemporary world of music. With his aloofness and astringency of style, his persistent austerity of temper, his invincible hatred of the sensuous, his detestation of the kind of "felicity" which is a goal for lesser men, this remarkable musician—who, far more deservingly than the incontinent Chopin, deserves the title of "the proudest poetic spirit of our time"—this remarkable musician, one must repeat, is the sort of creative artist who is writing, not for his day, but for a surprised and apprehending futurity. He is at once a man of singularly devout and simple nature, and an entire mystic. For him the spectacle of the living earth, in lovely or forbidding guise, evokes reverend and exalted moods. His approach to its wonders is Wordsworthian in its deep and awe-struck reverence and its fundamental sincerity. He does not, like his younger artistic kinsman, Debussy, see in it all manner of fantastic and mist-enwrapped visions; it is not for him a pageant of delicate and shining dreams. Mallarmé's lazy and indulgent Faun in amorous woodland reverie would not have suggested to him, as to Debussy, music whose sensuousness is as exquisitely concealed as it is marvellously transfigured. The mysticism of d'Indy is pre-eminently religious; it has no tinge of sensuousness; it is large and benign rather than intimate and intense.

He is absolutely himself, absolutely characteristic, for example, in his tripartite tone-poem, "Jour d'été à la montagne." This music is a hymn the grave ecstasy and the utter sincerity of which are as evident as they are impressive. In its art it is remarkable — not so monumental in plan, so astoundingly complex in detail, as his superb B-minor symphony, yet a work that is full of his peculiar traits.

Now it would seem as if so fastidious and individual a musician as this might do something of very uncommon quality if he once turned his hand to opera-making. Yet in his "L'Étranger," completed only a year before he began work on his astonishing B-minor symphony, and in his "Fervaal" (1889-95), we have the melancholy spectacle of M. d'Indy concealing his own admirable and expressive countenance behind an ill-fitting mask modelled imperfectly after the lineaments of Richard Wagner. In these operas (d'Indy calls them, by the way, an *action dramatique* and an *action musicale:* evident derivations from the "Tristan"-esque *Handlung*) — in these operas, the speech, from first to last, is the speech of Wagner. The themes, the harmonic structure, the use of the voice, the plots (d'Indy, like Wagner, is his own librettist) — all is uncommuted Wagnerism, with some of the Teutonic cumbrousness deleted and some of the Gallic balance and measure infused. These scores have occasional beauty, but it is seldom the beauty that is peculiar to d'Indy's own genius: it is an imported and alien beauty, a beauty that has in it an element of betrayal.

We find ourselves confronting a situation that is equally dispiriting to the seeker after valuable achievements in contemporary French opera when we view the performances of such minor personages as Massenet, Bruneau, Reyer, Erlanger, and Charpentier. They are all tarred, in a great or small degree, with the Wagnerian stick. When they speak out of their own hearts and understandings they are far from commanding: they are vulgarly sentimental or prettily lascivious, like the amiable Massenet, or pretentious and banal, like Bruneau, or incredibly dull, like Reyer, or picturesquely superficial, like Charpentier — though the author of "Louise" disports himself with a beguiling grace and verve which almost causes one to forgive his essential emptiness.

Modern Italy discloses a single dominant and vivid figure. In none of his compatriots is there any distinction of speech, of character. In that country the memory of Wagner is less imperious in its control; yet not one of its living music-makers, with the exception that I have made, has that atmosphere and quality of his own which there is no mistaking.

I have referred by implication and reservation to three personalities in the art of the modern lyric-drama who stand out as salient figures from the confused and amorphous background against which they are to be observed: who seem to me to represent the only significant and important manifestations of the creative spirit which have thus far come to the surface in the post-Wagnerian music-drama. They are, it need scarcely be said, Puccini in Italy, Richard Strauss in Germany, and Debussy in France. Yet these men built upon the foundations laid by Wagner; they took many leaves from his vast book of instructions, in some cases stopping short of the full reach of his plans as imagined by himself, in other cases carrying his schemes to a point of development far beyond any result of which he dreamed. But they have not attempted to say the things which they had to say in the way that he would have said them. They have been content with their own eloquence; and it has not betrayed them. No one is writing music for the stage which has the profile, the saliency, the vitality, the personal flavour, which distinguish the productions of these men. So far as it is possible to discern from the present vantage-ground, the future — at least the immediate future — of the lyric stage is theirs. In no other quarters may one observe any manifestations that are not either negligible by reason of their own quality, or mere dilutions, with or without adulterous admixtures, of the Wagnerian brew.

A VIEW OF PUCCINI

A VIEW OF PUCCINI

A PLAIN-SPOKEN and not too reverent observer of contemporary musical manners, discussing the melodic style of the Young Italian opera-makers, has observed that it is fortunate in that it "gives the singers opportunity to pour out their voices in that lavish volume and intensity which provoke applause as infallibly as horseradish provokes tears." The comment has a good deal of what Sir Willoughby Patterne would have called "rough truth." It is fairly obvious that there is nothing in the entire range of opera so inevitably calculated to produce an instant effect as a certain kind of frank and sweeping lyricism allied with swiftness of dramatic emotion; and it is because the young lions of modern Italy — Puccini and his lesser brethren — have profoundly appreciated this elemental truth, that they address their generation with so immediate an effect.

In those days when the impetus of a pristine enthusiasm drove the more intelligent order of opera-goers to performances of Wagner, it was a labour of love to learn to know and understand the texts of his obscure and laboured dramas; and even the guide-books, which were as leaves in Vallombrosa, were prayerfully studied. But to-day there are no Wagnerites. We are no longer impelled by an apostolic fervour to delve curiously into the complex geneaology and elaborate ethics of the "Ring," and it is no longer quite clear to many slothful intelligences just what Tristan and Isolde are talking about in the dusk of King Mark's garden. There will always be a small group of the faithful who, through invincible and loving study, will have learned by heart every secret of these dramas. But for the casual opera-goer, granting him all possible intelligence and intellectual curiosity, they cannot but seem the reverse of crystal-clear, logical, and compact. A score of years ago those who cared at all for the dramatic element in opera, and the measure of whose delight was not filled up by the vocal pyrotechny which was the mainstay of the operas of the older répertoire, found in these music-dramas their chief solace and satisfaction. Wagner reigned then virtually alone over his kingdom.

The dignity, the imaginative power, and the impressive emotional sweep of his dramas, as dramas, offset their obscurity and their inordinate bulk; and always their splendid investiture of music exerted, in and of itself, an enthralling fascination. And that condition of affairs might have continued for much longer had not certain impetuous young men of modern Italy demonstrated the possibility of writing operas which were both engrossing on their purely dramatic side and, in their music, eloquent with the eloquence that had come to be expected of the modern opera-maker.

Moreover, these music-dramas had the incalculable merit, for our time and environment, of being both swift in movement and unimpeachably obvious in meaning. Thereupon began the reign of young Italy in contemporary opera. It was inaugurated with the "Cavalleria Rusticana" of Mascagni and the "I Pagliacci" of Leoncavallo; and it is continued to-day, with immense vigour and persistence, by Puccini with all his later works. The sway of the composer of "Tosca," "Bohème," and "Madame Butterfly" is triumphant and wellnigh absolute; and the reasons for it are not elusive. He has selected for musical treatment dramas that are terse and rapid in action and intelligible in detail, and he has underscored them with music that is impassioned, incisive, highly spiced, rhetorical, sometimes poetic and ingenious, and pervadingly sentimental. Moreover, he possesses, as his most prosperous attribute, that facility in writing fervid and often banal melodies to the immediate and unfailing effect of which, in the words of Mr. Henry T. Finck, I have alluded. As a sensitive English critic, Mr. Vernon Blackburn, once very happily observed, Puccini is "essentially a man of his own generation . . . the one who has caught up the spirit of his time, and has made his compact with that time, in order that he should not lose anything which a contemporary generation might give him."

It is a curious and striking truth that the chief trouble with the representative musical dramatists who have built, from the standpoint of system, upon the foundational stones that Wagner laid, is not, as the enemies and opponents of Bayreuth used to charge, an excess of drama at the expense of the music, but—as was the case with Wagner himself (a fact which I have elsewhere in this volume attempted to demonstrate)—an excess of music at the expense of the drama: in short, the precise defect against which reformers of the opera have inveighed since the days of Gluck. With Richard Strauss this musical excess is orchestral; with the modern Italians it implicates the voice-parts, and is manifested in a lingering devotion to full-blown melodic expression achieved at the expense of dramatic truth, logic, and consistency. In this, Puccini has simply, in the candid phrase of Mr. Blackburn, "caught up the spirit of his time, and made his compact with that time." That is to say, he has, with undoubted artistic sincerity, played upon the insatiable desire of the modern ear for an ardent and elemental kind of melodic effect, and upon the acquired desire of the modern intelligence for a terse and dynamic substratum of drama. His fault, from what I hold to be the ideal standpoint in these matters, is that he has not perfectly fused his music and his drama. There is a sufficiently concrete example of what

I mean—an example which points both his strength and his weakness—in the second act of "Tosca," where he halts the cumulative movement of the scene between *Scarpia* and *Tosca*, which he has up to that point developed with superb dramatic logic, in order to placate those who may not over-long be debarred from their lyrical sweetmeats; but also—for it would be absurd to charge him with insincerity or time-serving in this matter—in order that he may satisfy his own ineluctable tendency toward a periodical effusion of lyric energy, which he must yield to even when dramatic consistency and logic go by the board in the process; when, in short, lyrical expression is supererogatory and impertinent. So he writes the sentimental and facilely pathetic prayer, "Visi d'arte, visi d'amore," *dolcissimo con grande sentimento:* a perfectly superfluous, not to say intrusive, thing dramatically, and a piece of arrant musical vulgarity; after which the current of the drama is resumed. We have here, in fact, nothing more nor less respectable than the old-fashioned Italian aria of unsavoury fame: it is merely couched in more modern terms.

The offence is aggravated by the fact that Puccini, in common with the rest of the Neo-Italians, is at his best in the expression of dramatic emotion and movement, and at his worst in his voicing of purely lyric emotion, meditative or passionate. In its lyric portions his music is almost invariably banal, without distinction, without beauty or restraint — when the modern Italian music-maker dons his singing-robes he becomes clothed with commonness and vulgarity. Thus in its scenes of amorous exaltation the music of "Tosca," of "Madame Butterfly" (recall, in the latter work, the flamboyant commonness of the exultant duet which closes the first act), is blatant and rhetorical, rather than searching and poignant. Puccini's strength lies in the truly impressive manner in which he is able to intensify and underscore the more dramatic moments in the action. At such times his music possesses an uncommon sureness, swiftness, and incisiveness; especially in passages of tragic foreboding, of mounting excitement, it is gripping and intense in a quite irresistible degree. Often, at such moments, it has an electric quality of vigour, a curious nervous strength. That is its cardinal merit: its spare, lithe, closely-knit, clean-cut, immensely energetic orchestral enforcement of those portions of the drama where the action is swift, tense, cumulative, rather than of sentimental or amorous connotation. Puccini has, indeed, an almost unparalleled capacity for a kind of orchestral commentary which is both forceful and succinct. He wastes no words, he makes no superfluous gestures: he is masterfully direct, pregnant, expeditious, compact. Could anything be more admirable, in what it attempts and brilliantly contrives to do, than almost the entire second act of "Tosca," with the exception of the sentimental and obstructive Prayer? How closely, with what unswerving fidelity, the music clings to the contours of the play; and with what an economy of effort its effects are made! Puccini is thus, at his best, a Wagnerian in the truest sense — a far more consistent Wagnerian than was Wagner himself.

It is in "Tosca" that he should be studied. He is not elsewhere so sincere, direct, pungent, telling.

And it is in "Tosca," also, that his melodic vein, which is generally broad and copious rather than fine and deep, yields some of the true and individual beauty which is its occasional, its very rare, possession—for example, to name it at its best, the poetic and exceedingly personal music which accompanies the advancing of dawn over the house-tops of Rome, at the beginning of the last act: a passage the melancholy beauty and sincere emotion of which it would be difficult to overpraise.

In Puccini's later and much more elaborate and meticulous "Madame Butterfly," there is less that one can unreservedly delight in or definitely deplore, so far as the music itself is concerned. It is from a somewhat different angle that one is moved to consider the work.

In choosing the subject for this music-drama, Puccini set himself a task to which even his extraordinary competency as a lyric-dramatist has not quite been equal. As every one knows, the story for which Puccini has here sought a lyrico-dramatic expression is that of an American naval officer who marries little "Madame Butterfly" in

Japan, deserts her, and cheerfully calls upon her three years later with the "real" wife whom he has married in America. The name of this amiable gentleman is Pinkerton — B. F. Pinkerton — or, in full, Benjamin Franklin Pinkerton. Now it would scarcely seem to require elaborate argument to demonstrate that the presence in a highly emotional lyric-drama of a gentleman named Benjamin Franklin Pinkerton — a gentleman who is, moreover, the hero of the piece — is, to put it briefly, a little inharmonious. The matter is not helped by the fact that the action is of to-day, and that one bears away from the performance the recollection of Benjamin Franklin Pinkerton asking his friend, the United States consul at Nagasaki, if he will have some whiskys-and-soda. There lingers also a vaguer memory of the consul declaring, in a more or less lyrical phrase, that he "is not a student of ornithology."

Let no one find in these remarks a disposition to cast a doubt upon the seriousness with which Puccini has completed his work, or to ignore those features of "Madame Butterfly" which compel sincere admiration. But recognition and acknowledgment of these things must be conditioned by an insistence upon the fact that such a task as Puccini has attempted here, and as others have attempted, is foredoomed to a greater or less degree of artistic futility. One refers, of course, to the attempt to transfer bodily to the lyric stage, for purposes of serious expression, a contemporary subject, with all its inevitable dross of prosaic and trivially familiar detail. To put it concretely, the sense of humour and the emotional sympathies will tolerate the spectacle of a *Tristan* or a *Tannhäuser* or a *Don Giovanni* or a *Pelléas* or a *Faust* uttering his longings and his woes in opera; but they will not tolerate the spectacle of a *Benjamin Franklin Pinkerton* of our own time and day telling us, in song, that he is not a student of ornithology. The thing simply cannot be done — Wagner himself could not impress us in such circumstances. The chief glory of Wagner's texts — no matter what one may think of them as viable and effective dramas — is their ideal suitability for musical translation. Take, for example, the text of "Tristan und Isolde": there is not a sentence, scarcely a word, in it, which is not fit for musical utterance — nothing that is incongruous, pedestrian, inept. All that is foreign to the essential emotions of the play has been eliminated. So unsparingly has it been subjected to the alembic of the poet-dramatist's imagination that it has been wholly purged of all that is superfluous and distracting, all that cannot be gratefully assimilated by the music. That is the especial excellence of his texts. Opera, though it rests, like the other arts, heavily upon convention, yet offers at bottom a reasonable and defensible vehicle for the communication of human experience and emotion. But it is not a convincing form, and no genius, living or potential, can make it a convincing form, save when it deals with matters removed from our quotidian life and environment: save when it presents a heightened and alembicated image of human experience. Thus we accept, with sympathy and approval, "Siegfried," "Lohengrin," "Die Meistersinger," "Don Giovanni"—even, at a pinch, "Tosca"; but we cannot, if we allow our understanding and our sense of humour free play, accept "Madame Butterfly," with its naval lieutenant of to-day, its American consul in his tan-coloured "spats," and its whiskys-and-soda.

This, then, was the prime disadvantage under which Puccini laboured. He was, as a necessary incident of his task, confronted with the problem of setting to music a great deal of prosaic and altogether unlovely dialogue, essential to the unfolding of the action, no doubt, but quite fatal to lyric inspiration. Under these circumstances, the music is often surprisingly successful; but it is significant that the most poetic and moving passages in the score are those which enforce emotions and occasions which have no necessary connection with time or place; which are, from their nature, fit subjects for musical treatment,—for example, such a passage as that at the end of the second act, where *Madame Butterfly* and her child wait through the long night for the coming of the faithless *Pinkerton;* for here the moment and the mood to be expressed have a dignity and a pathos entirely outside of date or circumstance.

The score, as a whole, compares unfavourably with that of "Tosca," which still, as it seems to me, represents Puccini at his most effective and sincere. In "Madame Butterfly" one misses the salient characterisation, the gripping intensity, the sharpness and boldness of outline that make "Tosca" so notable an accomplishment. "Tosca," for all its occasional commonness, its melodic banality, is a work of immense vigour and unquestionable individuality. In it Puccini has saturated almost every page of the music with his own extremely vivid personality: a personality that is exceedingly impressive in its crude strength and directness; he has, in this score, exploded the strange critical legend that his style is little more than a blended echo of the later Verdi, Ponchielli, and Massenet. The music of "Tosca" is not often distinguished, but it is singularly striking, potent, and original; no one save Puccini could possibly have written it. But since then this composer has, artistically speaking, visited Paris. He has appreciated the value of certain harmonic experiments which such adventurous Frenchmen as Claude Debussy, Maurice Ravel, and others, are making; he has appreciated them so sincerely that certain pages in "Madame Butterfly," as, for instance, the lovely interlude between the second and third acts, sound almost as if they had been contrived by Debussy himself—a Latinised Debussy, of course. Puccini, in short, has become intellectually sophisticated, and he has learned gentler artistic manners, in the interval between the composition of "Tosca" and of "Madame Butterfly." The music of the latter work is far more delicately structured and subtle than anything he had previously given us, and it has moments of conquering beauty, of great tenderness, of superlative sweetness. It is, beyond question, a charming and brilliant score, exceedingly adroit in workmanship and almost invariably effective. Yet, after such excellences have been gladly acknowledged, one is disturbingly conscious that the real, the essential, Puccini has, for the most part, evaporated. There are other voices speaking through this music, voices that, for all their charm and distinction of accent, seem alien and a little insincere. Has the vital, if crude, imagination which gave issue to the music of "Tosca" acquired finesse and delicacy at a cost of independent impulse?

STRAUSS' "SALOME": ITS ART AND ITS MORALS

STRAUSS' "SALOME": ITS ART AND ITS MORALS

THAT Richard Strauss the opera-maker is, for the present, summed up in Richard Strauss the composer of "Salome," would scarcely, I think, be disputed by any one who is sympathetically cognisant of his achievements in that rôle. Neither in "Guntram" nor in the later and far more characteristic "Feuersnot" is his essential quality as a musical dramatist so fully and clearly revealed as in his setting of the play of Wilde to which he has given a fugacious immortality. Yet in discussing this astonishing work, I prefer to consider it in and for itself rather than as a touchstone whereby to form a general estimate of Strauss the dramatical tone-poet; for I believe that, if he lives and produces for another decade, it will be seen that "Salome" does not furnish a just or adequate measure of Strauss' indisputable genius as a writer of music for the stage. I believe that he has not given us here a valid or completely representative account of himself in that capacity. So remarkable, though, is the work in itself, so assertive in its challenge to contemporary criticism, that it imperatively compels some attempt at appraisement in any deliberate survey of modern operatic art.

For any one who is not convinced that those ancient though occasionally reconciled adversaries, Art and Ethics, are necessarily antipodal, such a task, it must be confessed, is not one to be approached in a jaunty or easeful spirit, for it means that one must be willing, apparently, to enter the lists ranged with the hypocrites, the prudes, the short-sighted and the unwise; with frenzied and myopic champions of respectability; with all those who are as inflexible in their allegiance to the moralities as they are resourceful and tireless in their pursuit of impudicity in art. Yet that there are two standpoints from which this extraordinary work must be regarded by any candid observer I do not think is open to question: it has its purely æsthetic aspect, and its — I shall not say moral, but social — aspect. To separate them in any conscientious discussion is impossible.

Let us, to begin with, consider, in and by itself, the quality of the music which the incomparable Strauss — Strauss, the most conquering musical personality since Wagner — has conceived as a fit embodiment in tones of the tragic and maleficent and haunting tale of the Dancing Daughter of Herodias and her part in the career of the prophet John, as recounted — with non-Scriptural variations — by Oscar Wilde. We may consider, first, whether or not it achieves the prime requisite of music in its organic relation to a dramatic subject: an enforcement and heightening of the effect of the play ; setting aside, for the present, those other aspects of it which have so absorbed critical attention, and of which we have heard overmuch : its remorseless complexity, its unflagging ingenuity, its superb and miraculous orchestration. These are matters of importance, but of secondary importance. The point at issue is, has Strauss, through his music, intensified and italicised the moods and situations of the drama ; and, secondly, has he achieved this end through music which is in itself notable and important ?

Never was music so avid in its

search for the eloquent word as is the music of Strauss in this work. We are amazed at the audacity, the resourcefulness, of the expressional apparatus that is cumulatively reared in this unprecedented score. The alphabet of music is ransacked for new and undreamt-of combinations of tone: never were effects so elaborate, so cunning, so fertilely contrived, offered to the ears of men since the voice of music was heard in its pristine estate. This score challenges the music of the days that shall follow after it.

For the most part, the atmosphere of horror, of ominous suspense, of oppressive and bodeful gloom, in which the tragedy of Wilde is enwrapped, is wonderfully rendered in the music. There are beyond question overmastering pages in the score — music which has the kind of superb audacity and power of effect that Dr. Johnson discerned in the style of Sir Thomas Browne: "forcible expressions which he would never have used but by venturing to the utmost verge of propriety; and flights which would never have been reached but by one who had very little fear of the shame of falling." Of such quality is the passage which portrays the agonised suspense of *Salome* during the beheading of *John;* the passage, titanic in its expression of malignly exultant triumph, which accentuates the delivery of the head to the insensate princess; the few measures before *Herod's* patibulary order at the close: these things are products of genius, of the same order of genius which impelled the music of "Don Quixote," of "Ein Heldenleben," of "Zarathustra"; they are true and vital in imagination, marvellous in intensity of vision, of great and subduing potency as dramatic enforcement and as sheer music.

But when one has said that much, one comes face to face with the chief weakness of the score — its failure in the expression of the governing motive of the play: the consuming and inappeasable lust of *Salome* for the white body and scarlet lips of *John*.

> "Neither the floods nor the great waters can quench my passion. I was a princess, and thou didst scorn me. I was a virgin, and thou didst take my virginity from me. I was chaste and thou didst fill my veins with fire. . . . Ah! ah! wherefore didst thou not look at me, Jokanaan? . . ."

That is the note which is sounded

from beginning to end of the play — that is its focal emotion. And Strauss has not made it sound, as it should sound, in his music. When it should be wildly, barbarically, ungovernably erotic, as for the enforcement of *Salome's* fervid supplications in her first interview with *John*, the music is merely conventional in its sensuousness. It should here be febrile, vertiginous. But what, actually, do we get? We get a scene built upon a phrase in which is crystallised the desire of *Salome* for the lips of the Prophet; and this theme is saccharinely ardent and sentimental, rather than feverish and unbridled; a phrase which might have been a product of the amiably voluptuous inspiration of the composer of "Faust." The "Tannhäuser" Bacchanale, even in its original form, is more truly expressive of venereous abandon than is this strangely sentimentalised music. It has, no doubt, a certain effectiveness, a certain expressiveness; but the effect that is produced, and the emotion that is expressed, are far removed from the field of sensation inhabited by Wilde's remarkable Princess. Yet it would seem to be a point needing but the lightest emphasis that if the passion of *Salome* is not fitly and eloquently rendered by the music, the cardinal impulse, the very heart of Wilde's drama, is left unexpressed.

So it is in the music of the final scene, *Salome's* mad apostrophe to the severed head. Here we get, not the note of lustful abandonment which would alone remove *Salome's* horrible appetite from the region of the perverted and the incredible, but a kind of musical utterance which simulates the noble rapture of Wagner's dying *Isolde*. The discrepancy of the music in this regard has been recognised by those who praise most warmly Strauss' score.

It has been said in extenuation, on the one hand, that music is incapable of expressing what are called "base" emotions, and, on the other hand, that Strauss wished to exalt, to idealise and transfigure, this scene. To the first objection it may be said simply that it is based upon an argument that is at least open to serious question. It is by no means an evident or settled truth that music is incapable of uttering anything but worthy emotions, ideas, concepts. There is music by Berlioz, by Liszt, by Wagner, by Rimsky-Korsakoff, by Strauss himself, which is, in its emotional substance, sinister, demonic, even pornographic in suggestion; and not simply by reason of a key furnished by text, motto, or dramatic subject, but in itself—in its quality and character as music. But the claim need not be elaborated, or even demonstrated, since it is beside the point. One quarrels with the music of the final scene of "Salome" on the broad ground of its inappropriateness: because the emotional note which it strikes and sustains is one of nobility, whereas the plain requirement of the scene, of the psychological moment, demands music that should be anything but noble. And here we encounter the objections of those who hold that *Salome* herself, at the moment of her apostrophe to the dead head, becomes transfigured, uplifted through the power of a great and purifying love. But to argue in this manner is to indulge in a particularly egregious kind of fatuity. To conceive Wilde's lubricious princess as a kind of Oriental *Isolde* is grotesquely to distort the vivid and wholly consistent woman of his imagining; and it is to renounce at once all possibility of justifying her culminating actions. For the only ground upon which it might be remotely possible to account for *Salome's* remarkable behaviour, except by regarding her as a necrophilistic maniac, is that supplied by the conditions and the environment of a lustful, decadent, and bloodshot age. Only when one conceives her as frankly and spontaneously a barbarian, nourished on blood and lechery, does she become at all comprehensible to others than pathologists, even if she does not cease to impress us as noisome, monstrous, and horrible.

The music of "Salome," then, judging it in its entirety, is deficient as an exposition, as a translation into tone, of the drama upon which it is based; for it is inadequate in its expression of the play's central and informing emotion. One listens to this music, it must be granted, with the nerves in an excessive state of tension — it is enormously exciting; but so is, under certain conditions, a determined beating upon a drum. An assault upon the nerve-centres is a vastly different thing from an emotional persuasion; yet there are many who, in listening to "Salome," will need to be convinced of it.

It would be absurd to deny, of course, that "Salome" is in many ways a noteworthy and brilliant — and, for the curious student of musical evolution — a fascinating work. Its musicianship — the sheer technical artistry which contrived it — is stupefying in its enormous and inerrant mastery. The quality of its inspiration and its success as a musico-dramatic commentary, which have been the prime considerations in this discussion, have been measured, of course, by the most exacting standards — by the standards set in other and greater works of Strauss, in comparison with which it is lamentably inferior in vitality, sincerity, and importance.

In at least one respect, however, it compels the most unreserved praise; and that is in the case of its superlative orchestration. Strauss has written here for a huge and complicated body of instruments, and he has set them an appalling task. Never in the history of music has such instrumentation found its way onto the printed page. Yet, though he requires his performers to do impossible things, they never fail to contribute to the effect of the music as a whole; for the dominant and wonderful distinction of the scoring lies precisely in the splendour of its total effect, and the almost uncanny art with which it is accomplished. One finds upon every page not only new and superlative achievements in colouring, unimagined sonorities, but a keenly poetic feeling for the timbre which will most intensify the dramatic moment. The instrumentation, from beginning to end, is a gorgeous fabric of strange and novel and obsessing colours — for in such orchestral writing as this, sound becomes colour, and colour sound: it is not a single sense which is engaged, but a subtle and indescribable complex of all the senses; one not only hears, one also imagines that one sees and feels these tones, and is even fantastically aware of their possessing exotic and curious odours, vague and singular perfumes. It is when one turns from the bewildering magnificence of its orchestral surfaces to a consideration of the actual substance of the music, the fundamental ideas which lie within the dazzling instrumental envelope, that it is possible to realise why, for many of his most determined admirers, this work marks a pathetic decline from the standard set by Strauss in his former achievements. The indisputable splendour of this music, its marvellous witchery, are incurably external. It is a gorgeous and many-hued garment, but that which it clothes and glorifies is a poor and unnurtured thing. There is little vitality, little true substance, within this dazzling instrumental envelope; and for any one who is not content with its brave exterior panoply, and who seeks a more permanent and living beauty within, the thing seems but a vast and empty husk. It is not that the music is at times cacophonous in the extreme, that its ugliness ranges from that which is merely harsh and unlovely to that which is brutally and deliberately hideous; for we have not to learn anew, in these days of post-Wagnerian emancipation, that a dramatic exigency justifies any possible musical means that will appropriately express it: to-day we cheerfully concede that, when a character in music-drama tells another character that his body is "like the body of a leper, like a plastered wall where vipers crawl . . . like a whitened sepulchre, full of loathsome things," the sentiment may not be uttered in music of Mendelssohnian sweetness and placidity. It is because the music is so often vulgarly sentimental, when it should be terrible and unbridled in its passion, that it seems to some a defective performance. For sheer commonness, allied with a kind of emotionalism that is the worse for being inflated in expression, it would be hard to find, in any score of the rank of "Salome," the equal of the two themes which Strauss uses so extensively that they stand almost as the dominant motives in the score: the theme which is associated with *Salome's* desire to kiss the lips of *John*, and that other theme—it has been called that of "Ecstasy"—which begins like the *cantabile* subject in the first movement of Tschaikowsky's "Pathetic" Symphony, and ends—well, like Strauss at his worst.

An astounding score!—music that is by turns gorgeous, banal, delicate, cataclysmic, vulgar, sentimental, insinuating, tornadic: music which is as inexplicable in its shortcomings as it is overwhelming in its occasional triumphs.

We may now consider that other aspect from which, I have said, the candid observer is compelled to regard this remarkable work.

Those over-zealous friends of Strauss who have sought to justify the offensiveness of "Salome" by alleging the case of Wagner's "Die Walküre," and the relationship that is there shown to exist between the ill-starred Volsungs, are worse than misguided; for however unhallowed that relationship may be, it conveys no hint of sexual malaise. *Siegmund* and *Sieglinde* are superbly healthful and untainted animals: to name their exuberant passion in the same breath with the horrible lust of *Salome* is stupid and absurd.

Let us not confuse the issue: The spectacle of a woman fondling passionately a severed and reeking head and puling over its dead lips, is not necessarily deleterious to morals, nor is it necessarily an act of impudicity; it is merely, for those whose calling does not happen to induce familiarity with mortuary things, horrible and revolting. No matter how, in practice on the stage, the thing may be ameliorated, the fact,—the situation as conceived and ordered by the dramatist,—is inescapable. It has been said that this scene is not really so sickening as it is alleged to be, since the stage directions require that *Salome's* kisses be bestowed in the obscurity of a darkened stage. But to that it may be replied, in the first place, that darkness does little to mitigate the horror of the scene as conveyed by the words of *Salome* — so little, in fact, that *Herod*, who was anything but a person of fastidious sensibilities, is overcome with loathing and commands her despatch; and, secondly, that the stage directions expressly declare for an illumination of the scene by a "moonbeam" . . . which "covers her with light," just before the end, while she is at the climax of her ghastly *libido*.

Mr. Ernest Newman, a thoroughly sane and extremely able

champion of all that is best in Strauss, has said, in considering this aspect of "Salome," that "the whole outcry against it comes from a number of too excitable people who are not artists, and who therefore cannot understand the attitude of the artist towards work of this kind. Human nature," he goes on, "breaks out into a variety of forms of energy that are not at all nice from the moral point of view — murder, for example, or forgery, or the struggle of the ambitious politician for power, or the desire to get rich quickly at other people's expense. But because these things are objectionable in themselves and dangerous to social well-being there is no reason why the artist should not interest us in them by the genius with which he describes them. Stevenson's Dr. Jekyll-Mr. Hyde was a dangerous person whom, in real life, we should want the police to lay by the heels; but sensible people who read the story do not bristle with indignation at Stevenson for creating such a character; they simply enjoy the art of it. The writing of the story did not turn Stevenson into a monster of deception and cruelty, nor does the reading of it have that effect on us. Things are different in art from what the same things would be in real life, and an artist's joy in the depiction of some dreadful phase of human nature does not necessarily mean that, as a private individual, he is depraved, or that the spectacle of his art will make for depravity in the audience. Now Wilde and Strauss have simply drawn an erotic and half-deranged Oriental woman as they imagine she may have been. They do not recommend her; they simply present her, as a specimen of what human nature can be like in certain circumstances. . . . The hysterical moralists who cry out against 'Salome' . . . have a terrified, if rather incoherent, feeling that if women in general were suddenly to become abnormally morbid, conceive perverse passions for bishops, have these holy men decapitated when their advances were rejected, and then start kissing the severed heads in a blind fury of love and revenge in the middle of the drawing-room, the respectable £40 a year householder would feel the earth rocking beneath his feet. But women are not going to do these spicy things simply because they saw *Salome* on the stage do something like them, any more than men are going to walk over the bodies of little children because they read that Mr. Hyde did so, or murder their brothers because Hamlet's uncle murdered his."

Now that, of course, is iresistible. But Mr. Newman's gift of vivacious and telling statement, and his natural impatience with the cant of those who hold briefs for a facile morality, have here led him, as it seems to me, astray. To deny that an intimate and vital relationship exists between the subject chosen by an artist and its probable effect upon the public is to yield the whole case to those who hold that this relationship, in the case of the theatre (and, of course, the opera house), is merely casual and inconsequential: it is to yield it to the upholder of the stage as an agent of "relaxation," an agent either of mere entertainment or mere sensation. It is not unlikely that Mr. Newman would be the first to admit that, if the prime function of art can be postulated at all, it might be conceived to be that of enlarging the sense of life: as an agency for liberating and mellowing the spirit: as an instrument primarily quickening and emancipative. "The sadness of life is the joy of art," said Mr. George Moore. The sadness of life, yes; and the evil and tragedy, the terror and violence, of life: for the contemplation of these may, through the evoking of pity, nourish and enlarge the spirit of the beholder. But are we very greatly nourished by the contemplation of that which must inevitably arouse disgust rather than compassion? I do not speak of "morality" or "immorality," since there is nothing stable in the use or understanding of these terms. But those aspects of life which sicken the sense, which are loathsome rather than terrible — are they fit matter for the artist?

It is a much mauled and much tortured point, and I, for one, am not unwilling to leave the matter in the condition in which Dr. Johnson left the subject of a future state, concerning which a certain lady was interrogating him. "She seemed," recounts the admirable Boswell, "desirous of knowing more, but he left the matter in obscurity."

To return, in conclusion, to Strauss the musician: Where, one ends by wondering, is the earlier, the greater, Strauss? — the unparalleled maker of music, the indisputable genius who gave us a sheaf of masterpieces: who gave us "Don Quixote," "Ein Heldenleben," "Zarathustra," "Tod und Verklärung." Has he passed into that desolate region occupied in his day by Hector Berlioz, for whom a sense of the tragic futility of talent without genius did not exist—the futility of application, of ingenuity, of constructive resource, without that ultimate and unpredictable flame? Is not Strauss, in such a work as "Salome," but another Berlioz (though a Berlioz with a gleaming past)? Is he not here as one disdainfully indifferent to the ministrations of that "Eternal Spirit" which, in Milton's wonderful phrase, "sends out his Seraphim with the hallowed fire of his altar, to touch and purify the lips of whom he pleases"?

A PERFECT MUSIC-DRAMA

A PERFECT MUSIC-DRAMA

I

SOMEWHAT less than a century ago William Hazlitt, whose contempt for opera as a form of art was genuine and profound, observed amiably that the "Opera Muse" was "not a beautiful virgin, who can hope to charm by simplicity and sensibility, but a tawdry courtesan, who, when her paint and patches, her rings and jewels are stripped off, can excite only disgust and ridicule." It may be conceded that matters have improved somewhat since that receding day when Hazlitt, whose critical forte was not urbanity, uttered this acrimonious opinion. The opera is doubtless still, as it was in his day, ideally and exquisitely contrived "to amuse or stimulate the intellectual languor of those classes of society on whose support it immediately depends." Yet the shade of Hazlitt might have been made sufficiently uncomfortable by being confronted, half a century after his death, by the indignant and voluble apparition of Richard Wagner. To tell the truth, though, Wagner is scarcely the opera-maker with whose example one might to-day most effectually rebuke the contempt of Hazlitt. While the Muse which presided at the birth of the Wagnerian music-drama can certainly not be conceived as "a tawdry courtesan," neither can she be conceived as precisely virginal, persuasive by reason of her "simplicity" and "sensibility." Wagner, for all his dramatic instinct, was, as we are growing to see, as avid of musical effect, achieved by whatever defiance of dramatic consistency, as was any one of the other facile and conscienceless opera-wrights whom his doctrines contemned. The ultimate difference between him and them, aside from any questions of motive, principle, or method, is simply that he was a transcendent genius who wrote music of superlative beauty and power, whereas they were, comparatively speaking, Lilliputians.

Mr. William F. Apthorp, speaking of the condition of the Opera before Wagner's reforms were exerted upon it, observes that it "remained (despite the efforts of Gluck) virtually what Cesti had made it — not a drama with auxiliary music, but a *dramma per musica* — a drama for (the sake of) music." Now it was, of course, the passionate aim of Wagner to write music-dramas which should be dramas with auxiliary music, rather than dramas for the sake of music; yet it is becoming more and more obvious that what he actually succeeded in producing, despite himself, were dramas which we tolerate to-day only because of their transfiguring and paramount music. In view of recent developments in the modern lyric-drama which have resulted from both his theories and his practice, it may not be without avail to review certain aspects of his art in the perspective afforded by the quarter-century which now stretches lengtheningly between ourselves and him.

II

It is, of course, a truism to say that the corner-stone of Wagner's doctrinal arch was that music in the opera had usurped a position of pre-eminence to which it was not entitled, and which was not to be tolerated in what he conceived to be the ideal music-drama. He conceived the true function of music in its alliance with drama to be strictly auxiliary — an aid, and nothing more than an aid, to the enforcement, the driving home, of the play. As Mr. Apthorp has excellently stated it, his basic principle was that "the text (what in old-fashioned dialect was called the libretto) once written by the poet, all other persons who have to do with the work — composer, stage-architect, scene-painter, costumer, stage-manager, conductor and singing actors — should aim at one thing only: the most exact, perfect, and lifelike embodiment of the poet's thought." Wagner's chief quarrel with the opera as he found it was with the preponderance of the musical element in its constitution. If there is one principle that is definite, positive, and unmistakable in his theoretical position it is that, in the evolution of a true music-drama, the dramatist should be the controlling, the composer an accessory, factor—like the scene-painter and the costumer, ancillary and contributive. If it can be shown that in the actual result of his practice this relationship between the drama and the music is inverted—that in his music-dramas the music is supreme, both in its artistic quality and in its effect, while the drama is a mere framework for its splendours—it becomes obvious that he failed (gloriously, no doubt, but still definitively) in what he set out to achieve. It was his dearest principle that, in Mr. Apthorp's words, "in any sort of drama, musical or otherwise, the play 's the thing." Yet what becomes of "Tristan und Isolde," of "Meistersinger," of "Götterdämmerung," when this principle is tested by their quality and effect? Would even the most incorruptible among the Wagnerites of a quarter of a century ago, in the most exalted hour of martyrdom, have ventured to say that in "Tristan," for example, the play 's the thing? Imagine what the second act, say, divorced from the music, would be like ; and then remember that the music of this act, with the voice-parts given to various instruments, might, with a little adjustment and condensation, be performed as a somewhat raggedly constructed symphonic poem. The test is a rough and partial one, no doubt, and it is subject to many modifications and reservations. It is not to be disputed, of course, that here is music which is always and everywhere transfused with dramatic emotion, and that its form is dramatic form and not musical form ;

but is there to-day a doubt in the mind of any candid student of Wagner as to the element in this musico-dramatic compound which is paramount and controlling?

It should be remembered that what Wagner thought he was accomplishing, or imagined he had accomplished, is not in question. He conceived himself to be primarily a dramatist, a dramatist using music solely and frankly as an auxiliary, as a means of intensifying the action and the moods of the play; and this end he pathetically imagined that he had achieved. Yet it is becoming more and more generally recognised and admitted, by the sincerest appreciators of his art, that as a dramatist he was insignificant and inferior. Had any temerarious soul assured him that his dramas would survive and endure by virtue of their music alone, it is easy to fancy his mingled incredulity and anger. He was not, judged by an ideal even less uncompromising than his own, a musical dramatist at all. It is merely asserting a truth which has already found recognition to insist that he was essentially a dramatic symphonist, a writer of programme-music who used the drama and its appurtenances, for the most part, as a mere stalking-horse for his huge orchestral tone-poems. He was seduced and overwhelmed by his own marvellous art, his irrepressible eloquence: his drama is distorted, exaggerated, or spread to an arid thinness, to accommodate his imperious musical imagination; he ruthlessly interrupts or suspends the action of his plays or the dialogue of his personages in order that he may meditate or philosophise orchestrally. He called his operas by the proud title of "music-dramas"; yet often it is impossible to find the drama because of the music.

It was not, as has been said before,

that he fell short, but that he went too far; he should have stopped at eloquent and pointed intensification. Instead, he smothered his none too lucid dramas in a welter of magnificent and inspired music — obscured them, stretched them to intolerable lengths, filled up every possible space in them with his wonderful tonal commentary, by which they are not, as he thought, upborne, but grievously overweighted. Mr. James Huneker has remarked that Wagner was the first and only Wagnerite. As a matter of sober fact, he was one of the most formidable antagonists that Wagnerism ever had.

It appears likely that his lyric-dramas will endure on the stage both in spite of and because of their music. The validity and persuasiveness of "Tristan" and the "Ring" as music-dramas, as consistent and symmetrical embodiments of Wagner's ideals, seems less certain than of old. But the music, *qua* music, is of undiminished potency — it is still, regarded as an independent entity, of almost unlimited scope in its voicing of the moods and emotions of men and the varied pageant of the visible world; and it will always float and sustain his dramas and make them viable. Gorgeous and exquisite, epical and tender, sublimely noble, and earthly as passion and despair, it is still, at its best, unparalleled and unapproached; and, as Pater prophesied of the poetry of Rossetti, more torches will be lit from its flame than even enthusiasts imagine. Nothing can ever dim the glory of Wagner the conjurer of tones. His place is securely among the Olympians, where he sits, one likes to fancy, apart—a little lonely and disdainful. In his music he is almost always, as Arnold said of the greatest of the Elizabethans, "divinely strong, rich, and attractive"; and at his finest he is incomparable. No one but a master of transcendent genius, and the most amazingly varied powers of expression, could have conceived and shaped such perfect yet diverse things as those three matchless passages in which he is revealed to us as the riant and tender humanist, the impassioned lyrist, and the apocalyptic seer: the exquisite close of the second act of "Die Meistersinger," where is achieved a blend of magically poetic tenderness and comedy for which there are analogies only in certain supreme moments in Shakespeare; the tonal celebration of the ecstatic swoon of *Tristan* and *Isolde* in the midst of which the warning voice of the watcher on the tower is borne across an orchestral flood of ineffable and miraculous beauty; and that last passage to which this wonderful man set his hand, the culminating moment in the adoration of the Grail by the transfigured Parsifal — music that is as the chanting of seraphs: in which censers are swung before celestial altars. Of the genius who could contrive such things as these, one can say no less than that, regarded from any æsthetic standpoint at all, he is, as the subtle appreciator whom I have quoted said of a great though wayward poet, "a superb god of art, so proudly heedless or reckless that he never notices the loss of his winged sandals, and that he is stumbling clumsily when he might well lightly be lifting his steps against the sunway where his eyes are set."

III

As music-dramas, then, appraised by his own standard, the deficiency of Wagner's representative works must be held to be the subordination of the dramatic element in them to a constituent part — their music — which should be accessory and contributive rather than essential and predominant. This tyranny is exercised chiefly — and, let it be cheerfully owned, to the glory of musical art — through Wagner's orchestra: that magnificent vehicle of a tone-poet who was at once its master and its slave. Yet Wagner sinned scarcely less flagrantly against his most dearly held principles in his treatment of the voice. He conceived it to be of vital importance that in the construction of the voice-parts no merely musical consideration of any kind should be permitted to interfere with the lucid utterance of the text.

His singers were to employ a kind of heightened and intensified speech, necessarily musical in its intervals, but never musical at the expense of truthfully expressive declamation. Yet in some of the vocal writing in his later works he is false to this principle, for he not infrequently permits himself to be ravishingly lyrical at moments where lyricism is superfluous and distracting when it is not impertinent. Again he is too much the musician; too little the musical dramatist.

And herewith I come to a curious and interesting point. Mr. E.

A. Baughan, an English critic of authority, who has written with both courage and wisdom concerning Wagnerian theories and practices, entertains singular views concerning the nature of music-drama as an art form. "There must be no false ideas of music-drama being drama," he has asserted: "it is primarily music. The drama of it is merely," he goes on, "the motive force of the whole, and technically takes the place of form in absolute music"—a sentence which, one may be permitted to observe, would contain an admirably concise statement of the truth if the word "merely" were left out. Mr. Baughan is led by this belief to take the position that whereas, in one respect Wagner was, to put it briefly, too musical, in another respect he was not musical enough. He acknowledges the fact that in Wagner's combination of music and drama, the music, so far as the orchestra is concerned, assumes an oppressive and obstructive prominence; it indulges for the most part, he holds, in a "superheated commentary" which leaves little to suggestion, which is persistently excessive and overbearing; yet at the same time Mr. Baughan holds that

Wagner, in his treatment of the voice-parts, did not, as he says, "make use of the full resources of music and of the beautiful human singing-voice in duets, concerted numbers, and choruses." It is the second of these objections which, as it seems to me, contains matter for discussion. So far from being deficient in melodious effectiveness, Wagner's writing for the voice, I would hold, errs upon the other side. It would be possible to name page after page in the "Ring" and "Tristan" which is marred, from a musico-dramatic standpoint, by an excess of lyricism. It is a little difficult to understand, for example, how Wagner would have justified his admission of the duet into his carefully reasoned scheme; for if the ensemble piece — the quartette in "Rigoletto," for example — is inherently absurd from a dramatic point of view, as it incontrovertibly is, so also is the duet. Even the most liberal attitude toward the conventions of the operatic stage makes it difficult to tolerate what Mr. W. P. James describes as the spectacle of two persons inside a house and two outside, supposed to be unconscious of each other's presence, making their remarks in rhythmic and harmonic consonance. Yet is Wagner much less distant from the dramatic verities when, in the third act of "Die Meistersinger," he ranges five people in the centre of a room and causes them to soliloquise in concert, to the end of producing a quintette of ravishing musical beauty? Had he wholly freed himself from what he regarded as the musical bondage of his predecessors when he could tolerate such obvious anachronisms as the duet, the ensemble piece, and the chorus? The truth of the matter seems to be that if Wagner's music, in itself, were less wonderful and enthralling than it is, those who would fain insist upon a decent regard for dramatic consistency in the lyric-drama would not tolerate many things in the vocal writing in "Tristan," "Meistersinger," the "Ring" and "Parsifal" which are not a whit more dramatically reasonable than the absurdities which Wagner contemptuously derided in the operas of the old school. His vocal writing, far from being deficient in melodic quality, far from ignoring "the full resources of music and of the beautiful singing voice," is saturated and overflowing with musical beauty, and with almost every variety of melodic effectiveness except that which is possible to purely formal song. Mr. Baughan complains that the voice-parts have "no independent life" of their own. "In many cases," he says, "the vocal parts, if detached from the score [from the orchestral support] are without emotional meaning of any kind — the expression is absolutely incomplete." An astonishing complaint! For the same thing is necessarily true of any writing for the voice allied with modern harmony in the accompaniment. How many songs written since composers began to discover the modulatory capacities of harmony, one might ask Mr. Baughan, would have "emotional meaning," or any kind of expression or effect, if the voice part were sung without its harmonic support?

No; Wagner cannot justly be convicted of a paucity of melodic effect in his writing for the voice. He would, one must venture to believe, have come closer to realising his ideal of what a music-drama should be if, in the first place, he had been able and willing to restrain the overwhelming tide of his orchestral eloquence; and if, in the second place, he had been content to let his *dramatis personæ* employ, not (in accordance with Mr. Baughan's wish) a form of lyric speech richer in purely musical elements of effect, but one of more naturalistic contour, simpler, more direct, less ornately and intrusively melodic in its utterance of the text.

It would be fatuous, of course, to deny that there are passages in Wagner's later music-dramas to which one can point, by reason of their continent and transparent expression of the dramatic situation, as examples of a perfect kind of music-drama: which satisfy, not only every conceivable demand for fullness of musical utterance (for that Wagner almost always does), but those intellectual convictions as to what an ideal music-drama should be which he himself was pre-eminently instrumental in diffusing. In such passages his direct and pointedly dramatic use of the voice, and his discreet and sparing, yet deeply suggestive, treatment of the orchestral background, are of irresistible effect. How admirable, then, is his restraint! As in, for example, *Waltraute's* narrative in "Götterdämmerung"; the early scenes between *Siegmund* and *Sieglinde*, and *Brunnhilde's* announcement of the decree of death to the Volsung, in "Walküre"; and in "Tristan" the passage wherein the knight proffers to *Isolde* his sword; the opening of the third act; and the first sixteen measures that follow the meeting of the lovers in the second act — where the breathless, almost inarticulate ecstasy of the moment is uttered with extraordinary fidelity, only to lead into a passage wherein the pair suddenly recover their breath in time to respond to the need of battling against one of the most glorious but dramatically inflated outpourings of erotic rapture ever given to an orchestra.

But scenes of such perfect musico-dramatic adjustment are rare in Wagner. It is not likely, in view of his insuperable propensity toward musical rhetoric and his amazingly fecund eloquence, that, even if he had kept a more sternly repressive hand upon his impulse toward musical elaboration, he could have accomplished the union of drama and music in that exquisite and scrupulously balanced relationship which produces the ideal music-drama. That achievement had to wait until the materials of musical expression had attained a greater ductility and variety, and until the intellectual and æsthetic seed which Wagner sowed had ripened into a maturer harvest than was possible in his own time — it had to wait, in short, until to-day. For there are those of us who believe that the feat has at last been actually achieved — that the principles of musico-dramatic structure inimitably stated by Gluck in his preface to "Alceste" have been, for the first time, carried out with absolute fidelity to their spirit; and, moreover, with that cohesion of organism which Gluck signally failed to achieve, and with that fineness of dramatic instinct the lack of which is Wagner's prime deficiency.

IV

It is not every generation that can witness the emergence of a masterpiece which may truly be called epoch-making; yet when France — not the Italy of Peri and Monteverdi; nor the Germany of Gluck and Wagner — produced, doubtless to the stupefaction of the shades of Meyerbeer, Bizet, and Gounod, the "Pelléas et Mélisande" of Claude Debussy, it produced a work which is as commanding in quality as it is unique in conception and design.

It has been left for Debussy to write an absolutely new page in the eventful history of the opera. This remarkable composer is to-day regarded with suspicion by the vigilant conservators of our musical integrity — those who are vigorous and unconquerable champions of æsthetic progress so long as it involves no change in established methods and no reversal of traditions; for he has shown a perverse disinclination to conform to those rules of procedure which, in music as in the other arts, are held to be inviolable until they are set aside by the practice of successive generations of inspired innovators. He has, in brief, affronted the orthodox by creating a form and method of his own, and one which stubbornly refuses to square with any of the recognised laws of the game. He is nowhere so significant a phenomenon to the curious student of musical development as in his setting of Maeterlinck's drama. For the first time in the history of opera we are confronted here with the spectacle of a lyric-drama in which, while the drama itself holds without compromise the paramount place in the structural scheme, the musical envelope with which it is surrounded is not only transparent and intensifying, but, as music, beautiful and remarkable in an extraordinary degree. The point to be emphasised is this: that the postulate of Count Bardi's sixteenth century "reformers," formulated by Gluck almost two hundred years later in the principle that the true function of music in the opera is "to secon poetry in expressing the emotion and situations of the plot," has its first consistent and effective application in Debussy's "Pelléas et Mélisande." What the *Camerata*, and their successors, could not accomplish for lack of adequate musical means, what Gluck fell short of compassing for want of boldness and reach of vision, what Wagner might have effected but for too great a preoccupation with one phase of the problem, a Frenchman of to-day has quietly and (I say it deliberately) perfectly achieved.

His success is as much a result of time and circumstance and the slow growth of the art as of a preeminent natural fitness for the task. The Florentines, for all their eagerness and sincerity, were helpless before the problem of putting their principles into concrete and effective form, for they were hopelessly blocked by reason of the desperate poverty of the musical means at their disposal. Spurning the elaborate and lovely art of the contrapuntists, they found themselves in the sufficiently hopeless situation of artists filled with passionate convictions but without tools — in other words, they aspired to write dramatic music for single voices and instruments with nothing to aid them save a rudimentary harmonic system and an almost non-existent orchestra, and with virtually no perception of the possibilities of melodic effect. Their failure was due, not to any infirmity of purpose, but to a simple lack of materials. Of Gluck it is to be said that, ardent and admirable reformer as he was, and clear as was his perception of the rightful demands of the drama in any serious association with music, he failed, as Mr. Henry T. Finck justly says, to effect a "real amalgamation of music and drama," failed to strike out "a form organically connecting each part of the opera with every other." His unconnected "numbers," his indulgence in vocal embroidery, his retention of many of the encumbrances of the operatic machinery, are all testimony to a not very rigorous or far-seeing reformatory impulse. If, as Mr. Finck pointedly observes, he "insisted on the claims of the composer as against the singer, he did not, on the other hand, alter the relations of poet and composer. Such a thing as allowing the drama to condition the form of the music never occurred to him." A spontaneous master of musico-dramatic speech, he stopped far short of striking out a form of lyric-drama in which the music was really made to exercise, continuously and undeviatingly, what he stated to be "its true function." It would be absurd to dispute the fact that his sense of dramatic expression was both keen and rich; but it was an instinct which manifested itself in isolated and particular instances, and it was not strong enough or exigent enough to compel him to devise a new and more intelligent manner of treating his dramatic text as a whole.

Of the degree in which Wagner fell short of embodying his principles — which were of course in essence the principles of the Florentines and of Gluck — and the evident reason for his failure, enough has already been said. So we come again to Debussy. For it is a singular fact — and this is the point to insist upon — that this French mystic of to-day is the first opera-maker in the records of musical art who has exhibited the courage, and who has possessed the means, to carry the principles of the *Camerata*, of Gluck, and of Wagner to their ultimate conclusion. In "Pelléas et Mélisande" he has made his music serve his dramatic subject, in all its parts, with absolute fidelity and consistency, and with a rigorous and unswerving logic that is without parallel in the history of operatic art; we are here as far from the method of Richard Strauss, with its translation of the entire dramatic material into the terms of the symphonic poem, and with the singing actors contending against a Gargantuan and merciless orchestra (which is nothing, after all, but an exaggeration of the method of Wagner), as we are from the futile experimentings of the *Camerata*.

V

One cannot but wonder what

Hazlitt, who could not think of beauty, simplicity, or sensibility as qualities having any possible association with opera, would have said of a manner of writing for the lyric stage which ignores even those opportunities for musical effect which composers of unimpeachable artistic integrity have always held to be desirable and legitimate. There is an even richer invitation to the Spirit of Comedy in trying to imagine what Richard Wagner would have said to the suggestion of a lyric-drama in which the orchestra is not employed at its full strength more than three times in the course of a score almost as long as that of "Tristan und Isolde," and in which the singers scarcely ever raise their voices above a *mezzo-forte*. Debussy's orchestra is unrivalled in musico-dramatic art for the exquisite justness with which it enforces the moods and action of the play. It never seduces the attention of the auditor from the essential concerns of the drama itself: never, as with Wagner, tyrannically absorbs the mind. Always in this unexampled music-drama there is maintained, as to emphasis and intensity, a scrupulous balance between the movement of the drama and the tonal undercurrent which is its complement: the music is absolutely merged in the play, suffusing it, colouring it, but never dominating or transcending it. It is for this reason that it deserves, as an exemplification of the ideal manner of constructing a music-drama, the hazardous epithet "perfect"; for it is, one cannot too often repeat, a work far more faithful to Wagner's avowed principles than are his own magnificently inconsistent scores. In this music there is no excess of gesture, there is none of Wagner's gorgeously expansive rhetoric: the "Je t'aime,"

"Je t'aime aussi" of Debussy's lovers are expressed with a simplicity and a stark sincerity which could not well go further ; and it is a curious and significant fact that the moment of their profoundest ecstasy, though it is artfully and eloquently prepared, is represented in the orchestra by a blank measure, a moment of complete silence. This, indeed, is almost the supreme distinction of Debussy's music-drama : that it should be at once so eloquent and so discreet : that it should be, in the exposition of its subject-matter, so rich and intense yet so delicately and heedfully reticent. After the grave speech and simple gestures of these naïve yet subtle and passionate tragedians, as Debussy has translated them into fluid tone, the posturings and the rhetoric of Wagner's splendid personages seem, for a time, violently extravagant, excessive, and overwrought. To attempt to resist the imperious sway which the most superb of musical romantics must always exert over his kingdom would be a futile endeavour ; yet it cannot be denied that for some the method of Debussy as a musical dramatist will seem the more viable and the more sound, as it is grateful to the mind a little wearied by the drums and tramplings of Wagnerian conquests.

His use of the orchestra differs from Wagner's in degree rather than in kind. As he employs it, it is a veracious and pointed commentary on the text and the action of the play, underlining the significance of the former and colouring and intensifying the latter ; but its comments are infinitely less copious and voluble than are Wagner's— indeed, their reticence and discretion are, as it has been said, extreme. Debussy's choric orchestra is often as remarkable for what it does not say as for what it does. Can one, for example, imagine Wagner being able to resist the temptation to indulge in some graphic and detailed tone-painting, at the cost of delaying the action and overloading the score, at the passage wherein *Golaud*, coming upon the errant and weeping *Mélisande* in the forest, and seeing her crown at the bottom of the spring where she has thrown it, asks her what it is that shines in the water? Yet observe the curiously insinuating effect which results from Debussy's deft and reticent treatment of this episode—the *pianissimo* chords on the muted horns, followed by a measure in which the voices declaim alone. And would not Wagner have wrung the last drop of emotion out of the death scene of *Mélisande?*—a scene for which Debussy has written music of almost insupportable poignancy, yet of a quality so reserved and unforced that it enters the consciousness almost unperceived as music.

The discursive and exegetical tendencies of Wagner are forgotten; nor are we reminded of the manner in which Strauss, in his "Salome," overlays the speech and action of the characters with a dense, oppressive, and many-stranded web of tone. Yet always Debussy's musical comment is intimately and truthfully reflective of what passes visibly upon the stage and in the hearts of his dramatic personages; though often it transmits not so much the actual speech and apparent emotions of the characters, as that dim and pseudonymous reality,—"the thing behind the thing," as the Celts have named it,—which hovers, unspoken and undeclared, in the background of Maeterlinck's wonderful play. We are reminded at times, in listening to this lucent and fluid current of orchestral tone, of Villiers de L'Isle-Adam's description of the voice of his *Elen:* "... it was taciturn, subdued, like the murmur of the river Lethe, flowing through the region of shadows." This orchestra, seldom elaborate in thematic exfoliation, and still less frequently polyphonic in texture, is, for the most part, a voice that speaks in hints and through allusions. The huge and imperious eloquence of Wagner is not to be sought for here. Taine once spoke of the "violent sorcery" of Victor Hugo's style, and it is a phrase that comes often to the mind in thinking of the music of the titanic German. Debussy in his "Pelléas" has written music that is rich in sorcery; but it is not violent. In it inheres a capacity for expression, and a quality of enchantment in the result, that music had not before exerted — an enchantment that invades the mind by stealth yet holds it with enchaining power. In a curious degree the music is both contemplative and impassioned; its pervading note is that of still flame, of emotional quietude — the sweeping and cosmic winds of "Tristan und Isolde" are absent. Yet the dramatic fibre of the score is strong and rich; for all its fineness and delicacy of texture and its economy of accent, it is neither amorphous nor inert.

VI

Tristan and *Isolde*, in moments of exalted emotion, utter that emotion with the frankest lyricism; *Pelléas* and *Mélisande*, in moments of like fervour, still adhere to the unformed and unsymmetrical declamation in which their language is elsewhere couched. It is the orchestra which sings—which, passionately or meditatively, colours the dramatic moment. Wherein we come to what is perhaps the most extraordinary feature of this extraordinary score:

the treatment of the voice-parts. Debussy's accomplishment in this respect, justly summarised, is this: He has released the orchestra from its thraldom to the methods of the symphonic poem (to which Wagner committed it) by making it a background, a support, rather than a thing of procrustean dominance, thus restoring liberty and transparency of dramatic utterance to the singing actors. He himself has succintly stated the principles which guided him in his manner of writing for the voices in "Pelléas." "I have been reproached," he has said, "because in my score the melodic phrase is always found in the orchestra, never in the voice. I wished — intended, in fact, — that the action should never be arrested; that it should be continuous, uninterrupted. I wanted to dispense with parasitic musical phrases. When listening to a [musico-dramatic] work, the spectator is wont to experience two kinds of emotion: the musical emotion on the one hand; and the emotion of the character [in the drama], on the other. Generally these are felt successively. I have tried to blend these two emotions, and make them simultaneous.

Melody is, if I may say so, almost anti-lyric, and powerless to express the constant change of emotion or life. Melody is suitable only for the song [*chanson*], which confirms a fixed sentiment. I have never been willing that my music should hinder . . . the changes of sentiment and passion felt by my characters. Its demands are ignored as soon as it is necessary that these should have perfect liberty in their gestures as in their cries, in their joys as in their sorrow."

Now Debussy in his public excursions as a critic is not always to be taken seriously; indeed, it is altogether unlikely that he has refrained from demonstrations of exquisite delight over the startled or contemptuous comment which some of his vivacious heresies concerning certain of the gods of music have evoked. These published appraisements of his are, of course, nothing more than impertinent, though at times apt and sagacious, *jeux d'esprit*. But when he speaks seriously, as in the defence of his practice which I have just quoted, of the menace of "parasitic" musical phrases in the voice-parts, and when he observes that melody, when it occurs in the speech of characters in music-drama, is "almost anti-lyric," he speaks with penetration and truth. His practice, which illustrates it, amounts to this: He employs in "Pelléas" a continuous declamation, uncadenced, entirely unmelodic (in the sense in which melodious declamation has been understood). Save for a brief and particular instance, there is no melodic form whatsoever, from beginning to end of the score. There is not a hint of the Wagnerian arioso. The declamation is founded throughout upon the natural inflections of the voice in speaking — it is, indeed, virtually an electrified and heightened form of speech. It is never musical, for the sake of sheer musical beauty, when the emotion within the text or situation does not lift it to the plane where the quality of utterance tends naturally and inevitably toward lyricism of accent. He does not, for example, commit the kind of indiscretion that Wagner commits when he makes *Isolde* sing the highly unlyrical line, "Der 'Tantris' mit sorgender List sich nannte," to a phrase that has the double demerit of being "parasitically" and intrusively melodic and wholly conventional in pattern — one of those musical platitudes which have no excuse for existence in any sincere and vital score. Nor in "Pelléas" do the singers ever sing, it need hardly be said, anything remotely approaching a duet, a concerted number, or a chorus (the snatches of distant song heard from the sailors on the departing ship is a mere touch of atmospheric suggestion). The dialogue is everywhere and always clearly individualised, as in the spoken drama. Yet this surprising fact is to be noted: undeviatingly naturalistic as are the voice-parts in their structure and inflection, and despite their haughty and stoic intolerance of melodic effect, they yet are so contrived that they often yield — incidentally, as it were — effects of musical beauty; and in so doing, they demonstrate the unfamiliar truth that there is possible in music-drama a use of the voice which permits of an expressiveness that is both telling and beautiful, though it yields nothing that accepted canons would warrant us in describing as either melody or melodious declamation. Now Mr. Baughan, whose views concerning Wagner and his habits have been discussed, craves in the music-dramas of Wagner a frankness of melody in the vocal writing whose absence he deplores; and he seems to think that when this melodiousness of utterance is denied to the voices in modern opera, all that is left them is something "that an orchestral instrument could do as well"—something that, inferentially, is anti-vocal, or at least unidiomatic. It would seem that Mr. Baughan, and those who think as he does, fail to realise, as I have remarked before, the immensely important part which it is possible for modern harmony to play in the combination of a voice and accompanying instruments. It would not be difficult to demonstrate that a large part of what we are in the habit of regarding as a purely melodic form of vocal expression in the modern lyric-drama owes a large and unsuspected measure of its potency of effect to the modulatory character of its harmonic support. Take a passage that we are apt to think of as one of the most ravishingly and purely melodious in the whole of that fathomless well of lyric beauty, "Tristan und Isolde"—the passage in the duet in the second act beginning, "Bricht mein Blick sich wonn' erblindet." As one hears it sung by the two voices above the orchestra, it seems a perfect example of pure melodic inspiration; yet play the voice-parts, alone or together, without their harmonic undercurrent, and all the beauty, all the meaning, vanish at once: without the kaleidescopic harmonic color the melodic phrases are without point, coherence, or design. But this is aside from the point that I would make — that the potentialities of modern harmony make possible a use of the voice in music-drama which, while it is remote from the character of formal melody, may yet be productive of a kind of emotional eloquence that is exceedingly puissant and beautiful, and that may even possess a seemingly lyric quality. We find a foreshadowing of this kind of effect in such a passage as *Tristan's* "Bin ich in Kornwall?" where all of the haunting effect of the phrase is due to the modulation in the harmony into the G-major chord at the first syllable of "Kornwall." And one might point out to Mr. Baughan that this effect is subtly dependent upon the co-operation of the voice and the instruments. The phrase in the voice-part is not one "that an orchestral instrument could do as well," as Mr. Baughan would at once recognise if he were to play the accompanying chords on a piano and give the progression in the voice to a 'cello or a violin.

But while Wagner foreshadowed this manner of making his harmonic support confer a special character upon the effect of the voice-part, he did not begin to sound its possibilities. That was left for Debussy to do; and for the task he was obviously equipped in a surpassing degree by his unprecedentedly flexible, plastic, and resourceful harmonic vocabulary — the richest harmonic instrument, beyond comparison, that music has yet known.

The score of "Pelléas" overflows with instances of this — one may paradoxically call it harmonic — use of the voice: things that Wagner, with his comparatively limited harmonic range, could not have accomplished. As instances where the voice-part, without being inherently melodic, borrows a semblance of almost lyrical beauty from its harmonic associations, consider the passage in the grotto scene beginning at *Pelléas'* words, "Elle est très grande et très belle," and continuing to "Donnez-moi la main"; or the astonishing passage in the final love scene beginning at *Pelléas'* words, "On a brisé la glace avec des fers rougis!" or, in the last act, the expression that is given to *Mélisande's* phrase, "la grande fenêtre . . ." Yet note that in such passages the voice-part does not, in Mr. Baughan's phrase, merely "weave up" with the orchestra, as he protests that it does in Wagner's practice; in other words, it is not simply an incidental strand in the general harmonic texture; it has character and individuality of its own, though these are absolutely dependent for their full effect upon their harmonic background. Nor is it, on the other hand, so assertive and conspicuous that it comes within the class of that which Debussy repudiates as "parasitic." Here, then, is a method of uttering the text that not only permits of a just and veracious rendering of every possible dramatic *nuance*, but which, by virtue of the means of musical enforcement that are applied to it, takes on a character and quality, as music, which are as influential as they are unparalleled.

VII

It has been affirmed that in "Pelléas et Mélisande" Debussy has produced a work as commanding in quality as it is unique in conception and design. Let us consider what grounds there may be for the assertion.

To begin with, its spiritual and emotional flavour are without analogy in the previous history, not merely of opera, but of music. Debussy is a man of unhampered and clairvoyant imagination, a dreamer with a far-wandering vision. He views the spectacle of the world through the magic casements of the mystic who is also a poet and visionary. One can easily conceive him as taking the more tranquil part in that provocative dialogue put by Mr. Yeats into the mouths of two of his dramatic characters:

> "And what in the living world can happen to a man that is asleep on his bed? Work must go on and coach-building must go on, and they will not go on the time there is too much attention given to dreams. A dream is a sort of a shadow, no profit in it to anyone at all."
>
> "There are some would answer you that it is to those who are awake that nothing happens, and it is they who know nothing. He that is asleep on his bed is gone where all have gone for supreme truth."

In Maeterlinck's "Pelléas et Mélisande," Debussy has, through a fortunate conjunction of circumstances, found a perfect vehicle for his impulses and preoccupations. There will always be, naturally enough, persons who must inevitably regard such a work as that for which he and Maeterlinck are now responsible as, for the most part, vain, inutile, even preposterous. They are sincere in their dislike, these forthright and excellent people, and they are to be commiserated, for they are, in such a region of the imagination as this drama builds up about them, aliens in a world whose ways and whose wonders must be forever hidden from their most determined scrutiny. Such robust and worldly spirits, writes a thoughtful contemporary essayist, "that swim so vigorously on the surface of things," have always "a suspicion, a jealousy, a contempt, for one who dives deeper and brings back tidings of the strange secrets that the depth holds": they will not even grant that the depths are anything save murky, that the tidings have validity or importance. They take comfort in their detachment, and are apt to speak of themselves, with mock humility, as "plain, blunt persons," for whom the alleged vacuities of such an order of art are comfortably negligible. Well, it is, after all, as Maeterlinck's *Pelléas* himself observes, a matter not so much for mirth as for lament; yet even more is it a matter for resignation. There will always be, as has been observed, an immense and confident majority for whom that territory of the creative imagination which lies over the boundaries of the palpable world will seem worse than delusive: who will always and sincerely pin their faith to that which is definite and concrete, patent and direct, and who must in all honesty reject that which is undeclared, allusive, crepuscular: which communicates itself through echoes and in glimpses; by means of intimations, signs, and tokens. For them it would be of no avail to point to the dictum of one who, like Maeterlinck, is aware of remote voices and strange dreams: "Dramatic art," he has wisely said, "is a method of expression, and neither a hair-breadth escape nor a love affair more befits it than the passionate exposition of the most delicate and strange intuitions; and the dramatist is as free as the painter of good pictures and the writer of good books. All art is passionate, but a flame is not the less flame because we change the candle for a lamp or the lamp for a fire; and all flame is beautiful."

It is a dictum that is scarcely calculated to persuade a very general acceptance: a "passionate exposition of the most delicate and strange intuitions" is not precisely the kind of æsthetic fare which the "plain, blunt man," glorying in his plainness and his bluntness, is apt to relish. It is a point upon which it is perhaps needless to dwell; but its recognition serves as explanation of the fact that the music-drama into which Debussy has transformed Maeterlinck's play should not everywhere and always be either accepted or understood. For in the musical setting of Debussy, Maeterlinck's drama has found its perfect equivalent: the qualities of the music are the qualities of the play, completely and exactly; and, sharing its qualities, it has evoked and will always evoke the more or less contemptuous antagonism of those for whom it has little or nothing to say.

Of the quality of its style, perhaps the most obvious trait to note is its divergence from the kind of music-making which we are accustomed to regard as typically French. We have come to regard as inevitable the clear-cut precision, the finesse, the instinctive grace of French music; but we are not at all accustomed to discovering this fineness of texture allied with marked emotional richness, with depth and substance of thought — we do not look for such an alliance, nor find it, in any French music from Rameau to Saint-Saëns, Gounod, and Massenet. Yet Debussy has the typical French clarity and fineness of surface without the French hardness of edge and thinness of substance. The contours of his music are as melting and elastic as its emotional substance is rich; and it is phantasmal rather than definite and clear-cut; evasive rather than direct. His art, as a matter of fact, has its roots in the literature rather than in the music of his country. His true fore-bears are not Rameau, Couperin, Boieldieu, Bizet, Saint-Saëns, but Baudelaire, Verlaine, Mallarmé; and, beyond his own frontier, Rossetti and Maeterlinck. There is scarcely a trace of French musical influence in the score of "Pelléas," save for its limpidity of expression and its delicate logic of structure. The truth is that Debussy, with d'Indy, Ravel, and others, has made it impossible to speak any longer, without qualification, of "French" quality, or "French" style, in music; for to-day there is the French of Saint-Saëns and Massenet, and the French of Debussy, d'Indy, Duparc, Fauré, Ravel: and the two orders are as inassociable under a generic yoke as are the poetry of Hugo and the poetry of Verlaine.

But the essential thing to observe and to praise in this music is its astonishing, its almost incredible, affluence of substance: its richness in ideas that are both extraordinarily beautiful and wholly new. The score, in this respect alone, is epoch-making. Debussy is the first music-maker since Wagner to evolve a kind of style of which the substance is, so to say, newly-minted. Strauss is not to be compared with him in this regard; for the basis of the German master's style, upon which he has reared no matter how wonderful a superstructure, is compounded of materials which he got straight from Richard Wagner and his great forerunner, Franz Liszt; whereas the basis, the starting-point, of Debussy's style — its harmonic and melodic stuff — existed nowhere, in any artistic shape or condition, before him. To speak of it as in any vital sense a reversion, because it makes use of certain principles of plain-song, is mere trifling. Debussy is a true innovator, if ever there was one. He has added fresh materials to the matter out of which music is evolved; and no composer of whom this may be said, from Beethoven to Chopin, has failed to find himself eventually ranked as the originator of a new order of things in the development of the art.

VIII

Those who feel the beauty and recognise the important novelty of the music of "Pelléas et Mélisande" will for some time to come find it difficult to speak of it appreciatively without an appearance of extravagance. One owns, in trying to appraise it, to a compunction similar to that expressed by one of the wisest of modern critics, when, after applauding some notable poetry, he whimsically reminded himself that he "must guard against too great appreciation," and "must mix in a little depreciation," to show that he had "read attentively, critically, authoritatively." Well, there is no doubt a very definite risk in praising too warmly a masterpiece which has the effrontery to intrude itself upon contemporary observation, and upon a critical function which has but just compassed the abundantly painful task of adjusting its views to the masterpieces of the immediate past. I am quite aware that such praise of Debussy's lyric-drama as is spoken here will seem to many preposterous, or at best excessive. I am also aware that the mistaking of geese for swans is a delusion which afflicts generation after generation of over-confident critics, to the entertainment of subsequent generations and the inextinguishable delight of the Comic Muse — which, as Mr. Meredith has pointed out, watches not more vigilantly over sentimentalism than over every kind of excess. Yet I am willing to assert deliberately, and with a perfectly clear sense of all that the words denote and imply, that the score of "Pelléas" is richer in inner musical substance, in ideas that are at once new and valuable, than anything that has come out of modern music since Wagner wrote his final page a quarter of a century ago. The orchestral score is almost as long as that of "Tristan und Isolde"; yet in the course of its 409 pages there are scarcely half a dozen measures in which one cannot point out some touch of genius. The music is studded with felicities. One carries away from a survey of it a conviction of its almost continuous inspiration, of its profound originality. The score overflows with ideas, ideas that possess character and nobility, and that are often of deep and ravishing beauty — a beauty that takes captive both the spirit and the sense. It is difficult to think of more than a few scores in which the inspiration is so persistent and so fresh — in which there is so little that is *cliché*, perfunctory, derivative. Certainly, if one is thinking of music written for the stage, one has to go to the author of "Tristan" for anything comparable to it. It has been said that in this music Debussy is not always at his best, and the comment is justified. There are passages, most of them to be found in the interludes connecting the earlier scenes (which, it is well known, were extended to meet a mechanical exigency), wherein the fine and rare gold of his thought is intermixed with the dross of alien ideas. And it is equally true that the vast and wellnigh inescapable shadow of Wagner's genius impinges at moments upon the score: thus we hear "Parsifal" in the first interlude, "Parsifal" and "Siegfried" in the interlude following the scene at the fountain — the scene wherein *Mélisande's* ring is lost. But the fact is mentioned here only that it may be dismissed. The voice of Debussy speaks constantly out of this music, even when it momentarily takes the timbre of another; and none other, since the superlative voice of Wagner himself was stilled, has spoken with so potent and magical a blend of tenderness and passion, with so rare yet limpid a beauty, with an accent so touching and so underived.

The nature of Debussy's harmony, and the emphasis which is laid upon its remarkable quality by his appreciators, have provoked the assertion that the score of "Pelléas" is devoid of melody, or at least that it is weak in melodic invention. Of course the whole matter rests upon what one means by "melody." The comment is a perfect exemplification of that critical method which consists in measuring new forms of expression by the standards of the past, instead of seeking to learn whether they do not themselves establish new standards by which alone they are to be appraised.

The method has been applied to every innovator in the records of art, and it is probably futile to cry out against it, or to assert its stupidity. The music of "Pelléas" is rich in melody. It does not, as we have seen, reside in the voice-parts, for there Debussy, for reasons which have already been discussed, has deliberately and wisely avoided formal melodic contours. It is to be found in the orchestra — an orchestra which, while it depends in an unexampled degree upon a predominantly harmonic mode of expression, is at the same time very far from being devoid of melodic effect. But the melody is Debussy's melody — it is fatuous to expect to find in this score the melodic forms which have been made familiar to us by the practice of his predecessors,— men who themselves were made to bear the primeval accusation of melodic barrenness. Debussy's melodic idiom is his own, and it often baffles impatient or inhospitable ears by reason of its seeming indefiniteness, its apparently wayward movement, and because of the shifting and mercurial basis of harmony upon which it is imposed. It would be easy to instance page after page in the score where the melodic expression is, for those who are open to its address, of instant and irresistible effect: as the greater part of the scene by the fountain, in the second act; the whole of the tower scene — an outpouring of rapturous lyric beauty which, again, sends one to the loveliest pages of "Tristan" for a comparison; the affecting interview between *Mélisande* and the benign and infinitely wise *Arkël*, in the fourth act; the calamitous love scene in the park; and almost the whole of the last act. If Debussy had written nothing else than the entrancing music to which he has set the ecstatic apostrophe of *Pelléas* to his beloved's hair, he would have established an indisputable claim to a melodic gift of an exquisite and original kind. It has been said that he is "incapable of writing sustained melody"; and though just how extended a melodic line must be in order to merit the epithet "sustained" is not quite clear, it would seem that in this particular scene, at all events, Debussy may be said to have compassed even "sustained" melody; for the melodic line — varied, sensitive, and plastic though it is — is here of almost unbroken continuity.

In its total aspect as a dramatic commentary the score provokes wonder at its precision and flexibility. The manner in which each scene is individualised, differentiated and set apart from every other scene, is of a vividness and fidelity beyond praise. For every changing aspect of the play, for its every emotional phase, the composer has discovered the exact and illuminating equivalent. The eloquence of this music is seldom abated; it is as pervasive as it is extreme. One would not be far wrong, probably, in finding this music-drama's chief and final claim to the highest excellence in its triumphant character as an expressional achievement; in this it ranks with the supreme things in music. There are in the score innumerable passages which one is tempted to adduce as particular instances of ideally fit and beautiful expression. It is probably unnecessary to allege the quality of such examples as the scene by the fountain, the perilous encounter at the tower window, the final tryst in the park, or the interlude which accompanies the change of scene from the castle vaults to the sunlit terrace above the sea — music that has an entrancing radiance and perfume, through which blows "all the air of all the sea"— these things will be rightly valued by every observer of liberal comprehension and sensitive discernment: to name them is to praise them. But there are other triumphs of expression in the score whose quality is not so immediately to be perceived. I do not speak of the countless felicities of structural and external detail: felicities which will repay close and protracted study. I am thinking of remoter, less obvious felicities: of the grave beauty of the passage in which *Geneviève* reads to the King the letter of *Golaud* to his brother *Pelléas*[1]; of the extraordinary final measures of the first act, after *Mélisande's* question: "Oh! . . . pourquoi partez-vous?"; of the delicious effect which is heard in the orchestra at *Pelléas'* words, in the scene at the fountain, " . . . le soleil n'entre jamais"; of the exquisite setting of *Golaud's* exclamation of delight over the beauty of *Mélisande's* hands; of the entire grotto scene,—a passage of superb imaginative fervour,—with its indescribably poetic ending (the frag-

[1] As one out of many instances of similarly striking detail, observe the remarkable and moving progression in the voice-part from the D in the ninth chord on B-flat to the B-natural in the chord of G-sharp minor, at *Geneviève's* words " . . . tour qui regarde la mer."

ment of a descending scale given out in imitation by two flutes and a harp); of the passage in the tower scene where the two solo violins in octaves sing the ravishing phrase that accompanies the " Regarde, regarde, j'embrasse tes cheveux . . ." of the enraptured *Pelléas;* of the piercing effect of the *Mélisande* theme where it is combined with that of *Pelléas* in the interlude which follows the scene at the tower window; of the passage preceding the entrance of *Mélisande* and *Arkël* in the fourth act, where *Mélisande's* theme is heard in augmentation; of the passage in the transitional music following the misusing of *Mélisande* by *Golaud* where her theme is played by the oboe above an interchanging phrase in the horns — a *diminuendo* of inexpressible poignancy; of the impassioned soliloquy of *Pelléas* preparatory to the nocturnal meeting in the park; of the theme which is played by the horns and 'cellos as he invites *Mélisande* to come out of the moonlight into the shadow of the trees; of the exquisite phrase given out by the strings and a solo horn as he asks her if she knows why he wished her to meet him; of the interplay of "ninth" chords which is heard, in the final act, when *Arkël* asks *Mélisande* if she is cold, and the mysterious majesty of the passage which immediately follows, as *Mélisande* says that she wishes the window to remain open until the sun has sunk into the sea; of, indeed, the whole of the incomparable music of *Mélisande's* death; and finally, of that scene wherein the genius of the musician and musical dramatist is, as I think, most characteristically exerted: the curiously potent and haunting scene in which *Pelléas* and *Mélisande*, with *Geneviève*, watch the departure of the ship from the port and speak of the approaching storm. Here Debussy, in setting the simple yet elliptical speeches of the two tragedians, has written music which is of marvellously subtle eloquence in its suggestion of the atmosphere of impending disaster, of vague foreboding and oppressive mystery, which rests upon the scene. The penetrating "On s'embarquerait sans le savoir et l'on ne reviendrait plus" of *Pelléas*, sung over a lingering series of descending chords of the ninth; the strange, receding song of the departing sailors; the passage in triplets which is heard when *Pelléas* speaks of the beacon light shining dimly through the mist; the veiled and sinister phrase in thirds on the muted horns which follows the dying-away of the sailors' call: these are salient moments in a masterly piece of psychological and (there is no other word for it) subliminal delineation.

Whatever Debussy may in the future accomplish—and it is not unlikely that he may transcend this score in adventurousness and novelty of style — will not imperil the unique distinction, the unique value, of "Pelléas et Mélisande." It has had, it has been truly said, no predecessor, no forerunner; and there is nothing in the musical art that is now contemporary with it which in the remotest degree resembles it in impulse or character. That, as an example of the ideal welding of drama and music, it will exert a formative or suggestive influence, it is not now possible to say; but that its extraordinary importance as a work of art will compel an ever-widening appreciation, seems, to many, certain and indisputable. Thinking of this score, Debussy might justly say, with Coventry Patmore: "I have respected posterity."

NOTE

Some of the material contained in the foregoing studies appeared originally in articles published in *Harper's Weekly*, *The North American Review*, and *The Musician*. But for the most part the essays are new; and such passages of earlier origin as are retained have been considerably altered and amplified.